# Diary of

## for

## Women & Men

*An evocative, emotional journal designed to help you vent your frustrations, pour your heart out, stay organised & plan a brighter future*

*by*

*Tracey West*

# Diary of Divorce: for women & men

A catalogue record for this book is available
from the British Library.
This publication is not included under licences
issued by the Copyright Agency.
No part of this publication may be used in any form of
advertising, sales promotion or publicity,
unless agreed by the author beforehand.

Tracey West has asserted her right under the
Copyright, Designs and Patents Act 1988
to be identified as the author of this work.
Photography: Simon West
Design and Typesetting: Simon West

This is a First Edition of the paperback of
Diary of Divorce: for women & men
Copyright © October 2013 Tracey West
ISBN: 978-0-9575621-7-2

Published October 2013
By Magic Oxygen Publishing
www.MagicOxygen.co.uk
editor@MagicOxygen.co.uk

# Diary of Divorce: for women & men

I hope the emotionally charged pathway
this book invites you to tread
helps you carve an expedient route
through the trickier moments
then up and out the other side.

The dark days will end.

This book features advice already published as 'Poetry of Divorce: Coping Tips of the Day', via an App for Android devices available from the Google Play Store © Tracey West of Magic Oxygen Publishing, 2013. It is not designed to replace legal or medical advice and is simply there to supplement it. The author and publisher do not assume and hereby disclaim, any liability to any party for any loss, damage, or disruption caused by errors or omissions, whether such errors or omissions result from negligence, accident, or any other cause.

In other words, we cannot lay claim to curing all your divorce-flavoured ills, you will need to reach out and seek professional assistance, now more than ever before.

Printed by Lightning Source UK Ltd; committed to improving environmental performance by driving down emissions and reducing, reusing and recycling waste.

View their eco-policy at www.LightningSource.com

# Diary of Divorce: for women & men

The pages of this journal are waiting to be filled in by anyone who may be struggling as they prepare to leave their spouse and equally for anybody immersed in the mad mire of early separation and divorce.

It will help you keep a useful handle on the parties and organisations involved in your divorce proceedings.

Some of the entries might be emotionally easier to fill in after you receive your Decree Absolute.

As with any private journal, you are best advised to keep it locked away somewhere very, very safe.

All rights reserved. No part of this publication may be used other than for the purpose for which it is intended nor may any part be reproduced or transmitted, in any form or by any means, electronically or mechanically, including photocopying, recording or any storage or retrieval system without prior written permission from the publisher.

Requests for permission should be addressed to:-
The Editor, Magic Oxygen
editor@MagicOxygen.co.uk

Set in 11.5pt Times New Roman
Main headings set in Lovers Quarrel

## About the Author

Tracey West was born in London's East End in 1966. She started writing articles in 1995 and broadcasting in 2002, predominantly on downshifting, environmental topics and sustainable living.

In 2003 she founded InterNational Downshifting Week, a campaign designed to help people 'slow down and green up' and became an extremely proud Trustee for the National Association for Children of Alcoholics in 2006.

Under her previously married name of Smith, she penned the best-selling Book of Rubbish Ideas and was awarded an Honorary Fellowship to the RSA for her work promoting eco-matters at grass roots. Her most recent title is Poetry of Divorce: for women, a preview of which can be found at the end of this book. Her stance is pithy, earthy and essentially upbeat.

During her divorce, she suffered the usual bellyaches that come with the territory. She used a pen and notebook to lift herself out of the darkness by writing poetry; something she'd never done before. Poetry of Divorce: for women was the resulting work.

In 2011, she was made Patron of WAND (Women's Action Network Dorset) a group that helps countless women in crisis, strongly connected to the local women's refuge. Royalty donations from Poetry of Divorce: for women, are being made to both of these important organisations.

She is now a very happily remarried, work at home mum living in the South West, who agrees that the pen is far mightier than the sword and healthier than pies and pints.

## Other Titles by this Author

**Poetry of Divorce: for Women**
Tracey West, paperback & e-book
Paperback ISBN: 978-0-9575621-0-3
e-book ISBN: 978-0-9575621-1-0

**160 Divorce Coping Tips**
Tracey West, paperback & e-book
Paperback ISBN: 978-0-9575621-3-4
e-book ISBN: 978-0-9575621-4-1

**The Book of Rubbish Ideas**
Tracey Smith, paperback & e-book
Paperback ISBN: 978-1-906136-13-0
e-book ISBN: 978-0-9575621-2-7

**Deadhead the Roses**
Tracey West, paperback & e-book, coming 2014

**Poetry of Divorce: for Men**
Tracey West, paperback & e-book, coming 2014

Visit Tracey's website to keep up to date with news on these and other titles:

www.TraceyWest.co.uk

# Dedication

This book is lovingly dedicated
to them.

They both exposed me to
surprising levels of humanity
that I never knew existed.

Without their consistent
and reliable eye-opening
contributions to my work
none of these
adventures in my head
would ever have unfolded.

I have been truly blessed
by all they have done.

Thank you *so* much...

# How to Use This Book

I invite you to pick up your writing instrument as and when you feel like it and to work your way through this book, or idly flick to a page that calls you. Then simply lay out your thoughts.

On the pages of your precious and utterly unique journal, draw, scribble, yell, cry and detail your most optimistic hopes, your passionate and immediate needs and wants and start to write out the darkness that engulfs you as you progress through your divorce.

Above all, make the pages sing your story as you prepare to point your mind, body and soul towards a brighter future.

I can honestly say that everyone I've ever talked to about their divorce (believe me, there have been quite a few) has unfolded a completely different story.

No time scale has been the same, neither has the declaration in that all important box in the petition, where the poisoned blood of your marriage is spilled for the world to view in black and white.

Recovery periods from this staggeringly disturbing time in your life will remain just as volatile too.

Rather unsurprisingly, each and every one of your Diary of Divorce entries will take shape in much the same way.

Filling in the pages will proffer more reliable self-help than gin and crisps.

# THE STARTING BLOCKS

## WEDDING DAY DETAILS

YOU :

THEM :

WHO ELSE :

OUTFITS & COLOURS :

WHERE :

WHEN :

PARTY AT :

WEATHER :

WAS IT A GOOD DAY OR BAD OMEN? :

# Solicitorious

## Your Solicitor Contact Details

Name :
Firm :
Telephone :
Direct Dial :
Mobile :
Address :


– – – – – – – – – – – – – – – – – –

## Their Solicitor Contact Details

Name :
Firm :
Telephone :
Direct Dial :
Mobile :
Address :

# The Final Dawn

What do you recall of the day when the word 'Divorce' first reared its ugly head?

# The Ins & Outs

What have you decided
to tell your friends
about why you split up?

# Money Matters

List big expensive things like
car, house, boat
then with red & blue pens
circle who should get what

# Fur & Fins

How are your animals
going to be divided?

Who is Staying With You?

Who is Going to Live With Them?

# Dividing Lines

List contentious items to be split: gnomes, nice art, tea sets

Stuff I Want




Stuff I Really Don't Want




Stuff I Don't Want Them to Have
But I Don't Want Either

# YOU'RE SUCH A %*&?

## PEN THE WORST POSSBLE INSULTS YOU CAN MUSTER UP FOR YOUR EX

# ...STOP PRESS...

WHAT WAS IN THE NEWS ON THE DAY
YOUR DIVORCE PETITION WAS SERVED?

LOCAL

COUNTRY

WORLD

# Within These Walls

### Draw two houses :

In the first, shade in the
% of its value that you want

In the second, shade in the
% you eventually get

(both should be 50%)

# Critical DVD List

## Compile a list of the ones you absolutely must have

1)
2)
3)
4)
5)
6)
7)
8)
9)
10)
11)
12)
13)
14)
15)
16)
17)
18)
19)
20)

(that should be enough to rack your ex off sufficiently)

# Critical CD List

## Same thing, different flavour of shiny round plastic disc

1)
2)
3)
4)
5)
6)
7)
8)
9)
10)
11)
12)
13)
14)
15)
16)
17)
18)
19)
20)

(there's always the music section in the local library)

# A Mini-Bucket List

Ten achievable things you want to do once you're the other side of your divorce

1)

2)

3)

4)

5)

6)

7)

8)

9)

10)

# Sauce Pot

Who or what did you really think about while you were having sex with your ex?

(shopping – painting the ceiling – sleep)

# GET OUT OF THE HABIT

## LIST A SELECTION OF THEIR MOST DISGUSTING & REPULSIVE HABITS & REMEMBER YOU DON'T HAVE TO PUT UP WITH THEM ANY MORE

# Getting Cut Up About It

Sketch their favourite outfits
colour them in...cut them up
then shove your masterpiece
in the paper recycling

# Game Set & Match Up

## Who do you think your ex would be best suited to & why?

# Silver Screen Stars

If your life were a film
who would play you & your ex
& what happens at
The End?

# Single Threads

What are your predictions for their fashion changes?

# The Cat's Away

**What shenanigans do you think they will get up to once you are divorced?**

# Your Officially Allowed Profanity Page

Write down all the things
you wish you'd said to them
during the final showdown

# Short, Not So Sweet

*Write a few 6-word stories based upon your married life*

# Nuptial Night

## What do you remember most about your wedding night?

# Fundamentally Them

What will your abiding memories be
of their behaviour
& general disposition
first thing in the morning?

# HOW THE DIVISION BELL TOLLS

WHICH SIDE DO YOU THINK
YOUR FRIENDS ARE GOING TO FALL?

YOUR SIDE OF THE FENCE




THEIR SIDE OF THE FENCE

# Self-Affirmation Space

## Write down ALL the things that are AMAZING about YOU

**This is perhaps the most IMPORTANT page in the ENTIRE book**

# Dear Doctor

Name :
Surgery :
Telephone :
Address :

## Visit Log

When / Why / What Happened

# Caring Counsellor

Name :
Surgery :
Telephone :
Address :

## Visit Log

When / Why / What Happened

# Paper Power

## Continue Our List of Must-Read Books to Help You Through Your Divorce

1) Eat, Pray, Love: Elizabeth Gilbert

2) Poetry of Divorce for Women: Tracey West

3)

4)

5)

6)

7)

8)

9)

10)

# Cinematic Support

## Continue Our List of Must-Watch Movies to Help You Through Your Divorce

1) Love Actually

2) War of the Roses

3)

4)

5)

6)

7)

8)

9)

10)

# Tearful Tunes
## Continue Our Playlist of Self-Pitying Songs to Cry Your Heart Out To

1) I Want to Know What Love is: Foreigner

2) Everything I Do: Bryan Adams

3)

4)

5)

6)

7)

8)

9)

10)

# GET AWAY
## WHERE DO YOU FANCY GOING FOR YOUR FIRST PROPER BREAK POST-DIVORCE?

# Wise Up

Do you have any thoughts on furthering your education?

What Courses

When & Where Are They

# Sexual Non-Adventures

Pen humorous details of the
worst ever sex you
had with your ex

# Sticking Points

Score your ex out of 5 on anything from sex, housework, parenting, gardening, being human

Things they got a 1 in


Stuff they got a 2 in


Activities they got a 3 in


Events they got a 4 in


Bits they got a 5 in

# *Hot Under the Collar*

*Which of their friends have you
always secretly fancied
& what are you going
to do about it now?*

# Oh, Before I Go...

## Write out the fantasy conversations you wish you'd had on the day you parted

# Getting Well Soon

*Detail your medication programme as recommended by your doctor or counsellor & remember, there is nothing to be ashamed of*

When   /   What   /   Treating   /   Results

# SHUT THAT DOOR
## WHAT DO YOU FEEL YOU NEED FOR CLOSURE?

# Vicious Whispers

Create a list of rumours
it would have been fun
to spread about your ex

False Ones

True Ones

# The Bounce List

Name the top five people
you think they'll probably rebound with

1)

2)

3)

4)

5)

(and if they do, highlight them)

# Bury Their Treasure

Draw diagrams to show what you want to do with their prized possessions

# WHAT YOU'RE MISSING

## STICK A DREADFUL PHOTOGRAPH OF YOUR EX RIGHT HERE

# Cutting Remarks

## Make a collage of wedding photos
## & stick it here
## with honest remarks
## about the Bridesmaids & Best Man

# Master of Disaster

**Detail the worst decorating or DIY nightmares your ex was responsible for**

# A Fresh Lick of Change

What decorating plans do you have
for your ex-free bedroom?

(fabric – colour – texture - smell)

# **Vehicle Vengeance**

## **Use a thick pen to scrawl your famous last words on a photo or drawing of their car**

**(not the real car or you'll be in BIG trouble)**

# Food Freedom

List the foods you've always hated
& had to endure
but will never have to
cook or eat ever again

# Body Part Art

Draw their naked body
then add spots & boils to all the
places you'd like them to erupt

# Ring in the Changes

What are you going to do with your wedding ring?

# D-Day

## How are you planning to mark the day you receive your Decree Absolute?

# D-Day – Part 2

What did you actually do?

# Sweet Taste of Revenge

Document your deepest, darkest,
most vengeful thoughts

(remember, they're best kept on paper)

# I See This & Think of You

List items that have
painful associations
& state where they're headed

## Charity Shop


## Recycling Centre


## E-bay

# The Non-In-Laws

What did you really
think of their family?

# So Here's the Thing...

List the confessions you wish you'd been brave enough to tell your ex

# A Stick Face Like Thunder

Draw a selection of stick people to represent
your ex doing whatever they do
& emphasise abominable traits & features

# Final Whys & Wherefores

What was written in the
'Reasons For Divorce'
box in the Petition?

(what else should have been listed?)

# When Did That Happen?

*What were you doing when you realised you didn't love them any more?*

# Smashy Nicey

Draw pictures of any possessions of theirs you'd like to smash to smithereens

# The Wrong Attitude

What did your ex think about social topics such as politics, education, current affairs, music, booze, drugs & fidelity?

# Fibres of Truth

Draw their favourite clothes inside a virtual washing machine

Circle the desired settings
- boil - bleach - dye - tumble dry -
- shrink - throw a red sock in -
...START...

# Jekyll & Hiding

Describe the public face of your ex
then describe the reality
behind closed doors

# Yawwwwwwnnnnn...

Describe the most boring social event you ever had to endure in their company

# FACE OFF

## STICK A PICTURE OF YOUR EX HERE
## THEN HAVE GREAT FUN DEFACING IT

# IT'S A RIP OFF

## Cut or tear a piece from their favourite t-shirt & stick the snippet here

# More D-Days

## Log the timetable of your divorce here

Relationship ended :

Petition filed/arrived :

Court appearance :

Decree Nisi issued :

Decree Absolute issued :

Other notable events :

# A Page of Pure Grrrr

If you're feeling really angry about what's going on scribble your thoughts here

# If Only

Write out the things you wished you'd known before you married them

# Secrets & Lies

**Did you tell any lies
to cover your tracks
at the end of your relationship?**

# With This Initial I Thee Insult

Write their name out in full
& pen a cutting insult
starting with each letter

# Tissue Alert
If you're feeling deeply sad
about what's happening
pour your heart out here

# Back in the Saddle

*What attributes do you think you'll seek out in a new partner?*

# Snip Out the History

How might you like
to restyle your hair?

(stick a lock of it here)

# Further Down the Line

Do you have any positive aspirations
for you & your ex
once the dust has settled?

# Repeat Prescription
Pen a few pre & post divorce thoughts on getting married again

## Before

## After

# A FRIEND INDEED
## WHO HAS BEEN YOUR BEST FRIEND THROUGHOUT THE DIVORCE & HOW HAVE THEY HELPED YOU?

# Snakes in the Grass

**Aside from your ex has anyone projected unprovoked unexplainable unpleasant behaviour towards you?**

**(this may be an appropriate juncture to tell them to sling their hook)**

# Time Travel Permitting

In the early days of splitting up is there anything you wish you'd done differently?

# Anomaly Money

List the costs of strange items your divorce has run up

(sex toys, takeaway food, booze)

# A Lush New Love

If you have your eye
on a delicious new partner
who are they & why?

# A Stationary Log

List the dates where you did
nothing more
than stare at the wall

(they are often best served in pyjamas)

# Poetic License Granted

Pen a poem about how you feel
It doesn't have to rhyme
just shoot something from the heart

(seek out Poetry of Divorce: for women)

# HAVE IT & EAT IT

## SUGGESTED RECIPES FLAVOURS & COLOURS FOR YOUR DIVORCE CAKE

# Spill the Secret Beans

If you have any guilty secrets
that you kept from your ex
lay them bare here

# Mind of Elvis

Do you have any suspicions
about the general behaviour
of your ex before you split up?

# P-Arty Time

**Draw your ex naked
with detailed explanatory labels
for their most useless bits**

# It's All About You
List strengths you never realised you had until you split up

# THE MOVE MAKERS
LIST CONTACT DETAILS HERE FOR
LOCAL ESTATE AGENTS
RENTAL COMPANIES & REMOVAL FIRMS

# Revenge is Best Served Cold

Write out the fantasy recipes for the last meal you wish you'd served your ex

# Sud OFF

Celebrate by collating a list of their most awful items of laundry & remember you'll never have to handle them ever again

# One Last Try

Did your ex make any attempts at reconciliation?

# THE FINAL FLING

HOW DID YOU FEEL AFTER
YOU HAD THAT FINAL RUMBLE
IN BETWEEN THE SHEETS?

# TIME TO BRANCH OUT
## BUY A FRUIT OR NUT TREE
## TO REPRESENT THE NEW YOU
## DRAW IT & PUT THE GPS
## COORDINATES HERE

(SPEAK TO AV HARTWELL AT
TREEFLIGHTS.COM - A GOOD MAN)

# THAT BIT OVER THERE
## WERE THERE ANY
## PHYSICAL ATTRIBUTES
## ABOUT YOUR EX
## THAT YOU SIMPLY COULDN'T BEAR?

# THE 'D' LISTERS

## WHO IS ON THE GUEST LIST FOR YOUR DIVORCE PARTY?

# A Need to Know Basis

Inform the following of your change of circumstances as soon as possible

~

Bank / Building Society / Credit Card
Landlord / Mortgage Company
Council / Benefits / Inland Revenue
Child Benefit / CSA
Driving License / Passport
Nursery / School / College / University
Gas / Water / Electricity / Telephone
Insurance / Pension / Endowment / Health Care
Employer / Volunteer Organisations
Doctor / Dentist / Opticians / Chiropodist / Vet
HP & Credit Companies
Gym / Social Club / Magazine Subscriptions

(cross through them as you go & add any others)

# Sign Your Life Back In

If you are going to change your name practice your new signature here

# Bed Head

List the days where it hurt so much that you never actually managed to get out of bed

(then cut yourself some slack)

# A Sporting Chance

What sporty activities do you fancy trying out in your new life?

# Charitable Concerns

Have you ever wanted to do something amazing for charity?

(write it here & make it happen)

# Moving On

Where would you like
to move to & begin your new life?

(town, seaside, village, big city, suburbs)

# Bricks & Mortar

## Document details of the valuations of your property

(get at least three)

# End of Days

What has your pension
been valued at?




What has their pension
been valued at?




(be sure to check private & state)

# Fringe Benefits

## What money will you save by not being together?

**(think pub, club, gambling, habits)**

# Tattoo Taboo

Permanent body art is a bad idea right now
but body paint is just fine
what are you going to paint where
to celebrate your freedom?

# Safe Haven

If you need an urgent refuge
for you & your children
start here

**For Women**

England.Shelter.org.uk

Refuge.org.uk

WomensAid.org.uk

**For Men**

EsteemMen.co.uk

ManKind.org.uk

MensAdviceLine.org.uk

seek help
The National Domestic Violence Helpline is
**0808 2000 247**

# The Dark List

If you have been a victim
of domestic abuse
list dates & details here

stay safe
The National Domestic Violence Helpline is
**0808 2000 247**

# A Guiding Light

## Who inspires you & why?

(light a candle to send them love & thanks)

# SORRY SEEMS TO BE

Do you want to apologise to your ex for anything they didn't know you were responsible for?

# I Want One

Pick one big thing you were
never allowed to have
& make a plan to get it

# Banned Bands

Which band or singer were you prevented from seeing live?

(what's stopping you now?)

# The Young Ones

**What are your children's names
& how old were they
when you split up?**

# Innocent Thoughts

How have your children reacted to everything that's going on?

# Rightful Aid

## Child Benefit Contact Details & Log

Which Office :
Telephone :
Address :

---

Date / Time / What Happened










(you'll need your CHB Reference No)

# Young Fund Help

## CSA Contact Details & Log

Which Office :
Telephone :
Address :

---

Date / Time / What Happened




(you'll need your National Insurance No)

# Divorce Coping Tip of the Day

Write down any useful
coping mechanisms you've discovered

(Visit PoetryOfDivorce.com/coping
for a free daily burst of support)

# Sobering Thoughts

## Create a booze log & keep an eye on your consumption

# A Sweet Spot

## During your divorce what indulgences have you surrendered to?

# With Hindsight

What lessons have you learned about yourself
from being married?

# The Middle Line

## Mediator Contact Details & Log

Name :
Firm :
Telephone :
Direct Dial :
Mobile :
Address :

---

Date / Time / What Happened

# It's a Numbers Game

Calculate how many days

you were married then work out the

percentage you were unhappy

# I'VE HAD A FEW

## REGRETS ARE FUTILE
## IF YOU HAVE ANY
## LIST THEM HERE

# Previous Incarnation

Describe the person you were before you met & married your ex

# One For the Road

*Sex with an ex is rarely a good idea
Have you succumbed, how did you feel
& were you safe?*

# Source of Sauce

What toys of an intimate nature do you think you might order?

# The Last Word

List their most irritating words phrases & noises then rejoice in the fact that you'll never have to experience them again

Yippee!

# The End of Your End

Your marriage is over
Your essence is free
Be sure to keep this book
Under lock and key

Learn from what occurred
In the words penned above
And whatever you do do
Don't lose faith in love

# Divorce Coping Tip of the Day: The Free Android App

Our Divorce Coping Tip of the Day offers a free daily burst of uplifting inspiration delivered either by email, or to your Android mobile device.

The tips are aimed at women and men and offer advice on a wide range of practical and emotional topics.

You will also find many inventive distraction techniques to help you tread water through tricky times.

The tips cover a broad time frame and take you from leading up to leaving, during early separation, through your divorce and out the other side.

Scan our QR Code below with your Android device to download the application instantly, or visit our website at www.PoetryofDivorce.com/coping for the email version.

# A Preview of Poetry of Divorce: for Women by Tracey West

The first book to be published in this series is Poetry of Divorce: for women.

It's a completely unembittered collection of poetic fiction by Tracey West inspired by real women's stories and written during her own fractious divorce.

Endorsed by BBC Radio 4 regular performance poet Matt Harvey, it's a very grown-up read, gritty, dark in places and very saucy in others.

It covers the period of leading up to leaving, the dreaded solicitors, overcoming challenges you've never had to tackle before, financial nightmares, sex and other social experiments and on into new life.

Sales of the book help to raise money for the West Dorset Women's Refuge and Women's Action Network Dorset, two amazing organisations that help countless women in crisis.

Order a copy from your local independent bookshop or the usual Internet purchasing websites, or if you're feeling the pinch, request it from your local library.

# Poetry of Divorce:

## for Women

*An essentially upbeat collection of poems for women going through separation and divorce*

by
Tracey West

# Preface

Despite the aspersion-casting rumblings from the surrounding crowd, a divorce is only ever two people wide.

Your story is unique, as are your reasons for leaving, or the reasons your ex issued you with, as they slammed the back door on your marriage.

As the world turns unabated and oblivious to the fact that your universe now has a gaping hole in it, you have to cope with minutiæ and carve a route through to tomorrow and beyond. It can be arduous and exhausting on a cellular level, to put it mildly.

From personal experience, I'd say when you are in the thick of divorce, you feel like you're the only person going through it and of course, in a way, you are.

It's easy to think the pain will never end but it will eventually lessen. Then on some magical day, sometime in the unforeseeable future, your Decree Absolute will declare that there's nothing legal stringing you together and what a mixed bag of emotions that brings with it.

In the interim, you have to find coping mechanisms to deal with the invisible gossamer threads that conjoin you if you have children, or property to sell, or a business to run; it's not impossible, but it is rather uphill.

For me, reading and writing helped alleviate my angst enormously and a loaned copy of a love poetry anthology became a regular digest, so much so I had to buy it.

When I read Shakespeare's sonnets, or prose of love unrequited and ditties of dastardly divorces from centuries back, I realised that every heartbreaking scenario had been played out, countless times over.

I decided to put a purposeful light to my own darkness by writing poetry about the funny and dark sides of divorce. I wrote with pen and paper most days and sought out others in the same position who wanted to impart their bizarre stories to stoke my imagination further.

Before I knew it, an array of strange tales spilled from my shiny golden orange notebook, then aptly fitting chapter titles appeared and every painful word that fell out of my fingers, was like a loving kiss from a mother's lips on their child's grazed knee; this poem writing malarkey had healing qualities and for me, it was a blessing.

Many of the poems in this book have been penned with elements of somebody's truth in them, but as many have not. To be honest, sometimes I took the license to write poetry and did precisely that.

The chapters mark some of the key events that litter the long and winding road between parting company with the one you once loved and finding the new you.

I hope you enjoy them. I hope they move you and help you along your path through separation and divorce.

*Good luck on your journey,*

*Tracey x*

*If you are on the run up to leaving your soon-to-be-ex, be sure to compile a checklist of important documentation you need to take with you and tick every item off in turn.*

*Your birth certificate, your passport (and those for your children if applicable), also your driving license paperwork, key ID cards and papers, mortgage details, bank cards, cheque books and your marriage certificate, will be invaluable bits of paper in the months ahead.*

*You need your marriage certificate to file for divorce in the UK and I suspect in many other countries too.*

*It is possible to request certified copies of things, but it can be a costly affair and would throw unnecessarily delaying spanners in your works.*

*Coping Tip of the Day*

# Chapter 1
## Leading Up To Leaving

The countdown moments that draw you closer to leaving your partner are often poignant and highly memorable.

They also seem to sit in a timeless bubble and trying to motion through them feels like wading through knee-deep treacle in Wellington boots.

Incidents and altercations with them suddenly become emotionally palpable as your judgement is pushed to the limit and you ask and re-ask yourself those inevitable questions, "Am I at the end of my end? Can I do another day? Must I endure another year?"

It's an introspective analytical phase, liberally splashed with careful consideration of the consequences of what are probably going to be your ultimate actions.

It's difficult not to let outside influences permeate your decision making process and friends in the know may try to goad you into making a premature move for a variety of reasons. With hindsight, they may not prove to have been the most honourable of friends.

At the end of the day, the only person you have to justify your actions to is yourself. The day you decide to push that Big Red Button should be as firmly in your control as is humanly possible.

# I've Struggled Today

I've struggled today
The light's not been quite right
My eyelids felt heavy
And the room looked so bright

I've struggled today
To move far from this spot
I've a temperature, I'm sure
Oh so cold, then too hot

I've struggled today
There's something going round
Maybe flu is a-brewing
Don't you worry, I'm sound!

I've just struggled today
To find get up and go
Perhaps I'm doing too much
I should learn to say no

You'd have struggled today
If you'd been in my head
All the words rolled around
Could you be me instead?

Not forever, temporarily
'Til I get back on track
'Cos I've struggled today
And the kids are due back

They'll say, "Mum, have you moved?"
I'll say, "Course, I've been busy!"
I spun around doing nothing
'Til it made me feel dizzy

I've struggled today
And I'll struggle tonight
Must I really cook dinner
Cheese on toast is all right

I must peg the washing out
It's been sat there for days
I can smell it's gone musty
God, I've struggled today

I'm not even sure if I've been for a wee
I did boil the kettle, had two cups of tea
I'm not drowning in pity, that's just not for me
But I've struggled today to do much more than breathe

Oh woman, snap out of it!
Everything's falling apart
As I struggle to mend
My bruised and battered heart

No

For now I'll do sitting
Having quiet 'me' time
'Cos I've struggled today
Tomorrow, I'll be just fine

Lightning Source UK Ltd.
Milton Keynes UK
UKOW04f1613301013
220071UK00001B/5/P